Above All Else, Independence, Happiness and Success in Your Senior Years

Above All Else, Independence, Happiness and Success in Your Senior Years

Nancy D. Butler, CFP®, CDFA™, CLTC

Above All Else, Success in Life and Business

www.aboveallelse.org

ISBN: 0578190338
ISBN 13: 9780578190334

Contents

About the Author

DURING HER CAREER as a Certified Financial Planner® and Asset Manager, Nancy helped more than a thousand people manage their financial lives through the aging process. First, she helped them set goals for the retirement life they wanted and needed. Second, she ensured they would have the money they needed to fulfill their retirement goals. Third, she helped them through the financial aspects of aging including how to pay for the additional care they needed and preserve the assets they spent their lives building. Finally, she helped their families settle their estates.

Nancy also looked after her mother for twelve years, which gave her a greater opportunity to see firsthand many of the challenges of aging as well as the opportunities to make it the best it can be.

Now a senior herself, Nancy wrote this book to help people take greater control of what their future lives can be as they age. She will show you simple things you can do while your mind is sharp to enable you to potentially maintain your independence longer and live a more fulfilling life for whatever years you have left on this earth.

Nancy D. (Hollandersky) Butler
December 2016

Introduction

IT HAS BEEN confirmed that what people do, and what happens to them before they become old, is probably the most important influence on independence in their old age. You can enhance your chances of retaining independence by having a successful, healthy, and active life before and after reaching old age. Fitness, health, an active mind, sound financial resources, good self-esteem, and good relationships with family and friends are all associated with being able to stay and live independently. Even when serious disability or illness occurs, this can increase your choices and enhance the likelihood that you will be able to access services, be supported informally, and stay active while living independently. From the perspective of habits and confidence, older people are more likely to be active and happy in retirement if this has been the case earlier in life.

Over the last several years, older adults have been the fastest-growing segment of the American population. As we age, our ability to manage change can become more difficult. While your mind is still sharp and you can make good decisions for yourself, it is important to take time now to make the changes necessary to enable you to maintain your independence and happiness as long as possible.

This book provides specific steps you can take today and over the next several years to better ensure you are doing everything you can to have the life you really want for the rest of your days. These steps can also help you organize your life in a way that will make it easier for your loved ones when the time comes when you need their assistance, as well as making it easier for them regarding all the things they will need to deal with after you are gone.

Consider This

When you are at the end of your life looking back, how will you feel about the life you lived and how you treated others? What can you do differently starting today to ensure that, during whatever years you have left on this earth, you will be able to look back and feel great about how you lived your life beginning today and for the rest of your life?

The Definition of Retirement

SOME PEOPLE SAY they will never fully retire. They don't see themselves puttering around the house for the rest of their lives. They want to always be working in some capacity.

My definition of retirement is a time where you have your assets and income working for you properly in a way that provides enough income to comfortably support you for the rest of your life. If you are working, it is only because you enjoy what you are doing, but you can stop at any time and still be very financially comfortable. That is my definition of true retirement.

If you do not plan for my definition of retirement, at some point you may be forced to stop working due to ill health or other reasons. This may happen at a time when you are not financially able to handle it. Planning now can help ensure you are in the best position possible.

Six of My Rules of Thumb

1. Money you need in the next five years should not be in the market

    Maintain enough money in savings, checking, money market, and/or short-term certificates of deposit to cover the money you will need for the next five years. Investments that are more aggressive are inappropriate for short-term needs.

2. Take only the amount of risk you need to accomplish your goals

    Now that you are retired, the degree of risk you need to take with your investments is most likely lower than when you were working. During retirement, invest at the lowest risk level you can that enables you to still achieve your income and lump sum goals.

3. General rule of thumb: For the amount of income you can expect from a properly diversified portfolio and have the money last the rest of your life

   Do you know the amount of income you can take from your investments and ensure the money will last for the rest of your life? The percentage changes over time, but today it is about 3 percent. For example, if you have $350,000 of invested assets at 3 percent, you can withdraw $10,500 per year or $875 per month and reasonably expect the income to not run out before you do.

4. Will, trust, power of attorney, health-care power

   Talk with an estate planning attorney about drafting a will, power of attorney, health-care powers, and any other documents the attorney recommends. Once you have all recommended documents in place, they should be reviewed every three years even if nothing has changed in your life. Update them sooner if changes do occur. There is more detailed information about this later in this book.

5. First goal: Provide the income you need for the quality of life you want for the rest of your life

   My first concern in retirement for you has nothing to do with your children, grandchildren, or others. My first concern is ensuring that you have the income you need for the rest of your life to live comfortably for whatever years you have left on this earth.

6. Second goal: Use what you don't need to accomplish the first goal to preserve what you spent your life building so you don't lose it all in the last few years

If you have the income you need to live the life you want for the rest of your life, then I want it all for you. That means taking a portion of the income you don't need for a comfortable retirement and use it to preserve what you have spent your life building so that it transfers as intact as possible to the people you want it to go to instead of potentially losing it to taxes or the cost of long-term care.

But if the cost of the second goal cuts into the first goal, then consider forgetting about or reducing the second goal.

Important: Be sure to discuss all financial issues with your financial professional, all legal issues with your attorney, and all tax issues with your tax adviser before making any changes.

Making Great Memories: Low-Cost, Unique Ways to Preserve and Pass on Great Memories to Your Heirs

Our Memories of You

FOR PEOPLE WHO seem to have everything, it can be really difficult to find a great gift. Here is a low-cost way to put happy tears in their eyes.

- Purchase paper that is fancy on one side and blank on the other side, and cut it into five-by-one-inch strips.
- Send six of these strips in an envelope to each family member and friend of the gift recipient.
- Include a note explaining what to do. Ask them to do the following:

- Write a memory they have of the person the gift is for (one memory per strip).
- Then sign, date, and return each slip to you by the stated deadline.
- Purchase a box, urn, or another fancy container.
- Fold each strip and put the strips in the container.
- Wrap the gift as usual.

For my mother's eightieth birthday, I did this for her. I purchased a gold plate and had it engraved "Our Memories of You." I then attached the engraved plate to a beautiful mahogany box.

One relative reminded her of nicknames they had for each other years ago. Another talked about a special memory of her at the beach. Everyone did a great job writing a fun, funny, or upbeat memory they had of my mother. I compiled more than one hundred responses. She cried with joy as she read each one. She kept the box on the living room coffee table. She was proud to display it for all to see, and it was a great pickup for her whenever she needed a smile.

More Great Memories: Start a New Family Tradition

Now is a great time to make great memories with your family and friends. You could start a new tradition or just step out of your normal everyday life and do something out of the box and exciting.

We are all familiar with making a gingerbread house for the holidays. For fifteen years, I worked with my grandchildren on a different take on the traditional gingerbread house. Instead, we made haunted gingerbread houses in October. Each grandchild made his or her own. Then we went outdoors and collected colorful leaves to make the graveyard around the houses they made. Pretzel sticks and frosting were used to make spooky trees for the yard. It was a tradition we looked forward to every year. Of course, I took lots of pictures and scrapbooked them all. It's a memory we will have for the rest of our lives.

Haunted Gingerbread Houses

Another adventure to consider is a family cruise. Our family gathered from all over the country and took a week-long cruise together. With so many different personalities and likes and dislikes, it made it easy for everyone to find something on and off the ship to have a great time.

What can you do now to make more great memories? Don't be afraid to step out of your comfort zone and try something different. It can be invigorating and bring some of the best memories of your life.

Capture the Rich History of Senior Family Members and Yourself

Our seniors have a lifetime of history to share. Once they are gone, their knowledge and wisdom are gone with them. Learn from them now and pass on your family history and all the wisdom and memories they hold. It can make them feel important and valued and will be a memory you will cherish for the rest of your life and pass on to those after you. Here's another idea I did with my mother that was extremely meaningful and successful.

I provided my mother with approximately one hundred written questions and asked her to select ten to twelve questions and write her answer down for each question she chose. I entered all of her answers into the computer and printed a document with only the questions and answers she selected. I gave her the printed list to study and make any edits.

Once she was reasonably comfortable with what she wanted to say, I hired a professional videographer, like you would for a wedding. Before we began, my mother had her hair professionally cut and styled. She had a manicure and bought a new outfit. We then made sure we had a beautiful chair for her to sit in and that everything behind where she would sit looked great.

When we recorded the video shoot, I read each question to her and then prompted her with the answer she wanted to talk about. There were questions about her childhood, how she met my father, how he proposed to her, how she chose her children's names, her favorite memories, favorite songs, and so much more. We ended the video with the final question asking her what her family could do for her now.

After we were done shooting the video, I worked with the videographer to edit me out, so all you saw or heard was my mother. It turned out to be about a twenty-minute finished video. Later that year, I sent copies of the video to every family member as a gift.

Here are a few pointers for making a great video:

- Be aware of the visual behind the subject.
- This is a time they may want to look their best. Consider hair, nails, makeup, and a new outfit. Or they may want to just be themselves as they are normally seen.
- Ask questions in advance and jot down their answers so you can cue them on what they wanted to say.
- Keep it upbeat, but keep it real.
- I researched the family tree and added it to the cover of the video. You may want to do the same.
- You can hire a professional videographer or do it yourself.

This is a memory you will cherish for the rest of your life and pass on to those after you. A list of questions to consider is at the end of this book.

Taking Calculated Risk for a Better Life

It can be easy to let ourselves become sedate as we age. We get comfortable with our surroundings and become fearful of the unknown. Taking calculated risks can bring invigorating success. Think about the following:

- What excites you?
- What have you always wanted to do but haven't done yet?
- What fear would you like to overcome?
- Who should you make up with?
- Who have you lost touch with and need to reconnect with?
- What's on your bucket list?

Recognize That Life Is a Journey, Not a Destination

Living your life to the fullest is a process that will take you your whole life to develop. Don't get frustrated if it takes you a while to learn some things or if you experience setbacks. Life is a journey, not a destination.

Ask your local AAA office for ideas and research online resources for access to opportunities you may not have thought of but would find interesting or exciting and something you would like to experience.

One online resource is Cloud Nine Living. Its goal is to enhance people's lives through memorable experiences. Check it out at http://www.cloud9living.com.

How I Took Calculated Risk for a Better Life

When I was sixty-two years old, I flew to South Africa and went in the ocean on a shark cage dive with my daughter. While in South Africa, I also lay down with a live full-grown cheetah and pet him.

Was I afraid? Of course I was. But I would not let fear keep me from experiencing what turned out to be one of the most invigorating and memorable experiences of my life.

At age sixty-five, I flew to Israel for a two-week vacation with five people I didn't know. I met wonderful people and experienced a culture like no other. I rode on a camel, swam in the Dead Sea, kayaked on the Jordan River, and had one of the best trips of my life.

Shark-cage dive in Cape Town, South Africa

Petting a full-grown cheetah in
Durban, South Africa

My husband is not as adventurous as I am, and the grandkids want to stay home on their electronics. I strongly encourage them to step out of their comfort zone and try things. Sometimes without their knowledge of what they would be doing, I have gotten them to try things they have never done before that I knew they wouldn't do on their own, and they ended up loving it.

My youngest daughter loves adventure. It has been a great way for us to connect. She was with me on the shark cage dive and lying down with the cheetah.

Don't let fear keep you from living a full life. I am not saying you have to be as adventurous as I am. But find something new and exciting to you, and go out and experience it. Make life exciting and fun while making good memories.

Here are some of the other things I have done that you may want to consider:

- Beluga whale encounter at the aquarium
- Ride a Segway through a scenic part of a distant town
- Riding an elephant at the fair
- Swimming with dolphins
- Letterboxing in different parts of the country
- Travel—local, the United States, and the world
- Hot air balloon ride
- Parasailing
- Ride in a sailplane (it has no engine)
- Panda encounter at the zoo
- Indoor skydiving

- Swimming with stingrays
- Penguin encounter at the aquarium
- Special shows: Cirque du Soleil, circus, other cultural arts
- Special charity events

Below are still other activities to consider:

- Ride a zip line
- Stock car racing
- Scrapbooking
- Vacation at a dude ranch
- Travel to an exotic location

Riding a camel in Israel

Riding Segways with the
grandchildren, Mystic, CT.

Swimming with a dolphin

In the water with a beluga whale

Make it a point to do something bold every week. Step out of your comfort zone, even if it's for only a few minutes. This might mean talking to someone whom you generally wouldn't talk to or starting a project that you feel intimidated by. The more you're willing to challenge yourself, the more comfortable you will become with new experiences.

Learn something new. Pick a topic, preferably something you know nothing about and learn something about it. You can take a class or read an instruction book, newspaper, or Wikipedia. Then share what you've learned.

Make it a habit to learn something new on a regular basis. It can be weekly, monthly, or any other time frame, but make it happen. Just because we are getting older doesn't mean we no longer learn and grow or need to live in the past. Continual exposure to new things can keep us feeling happier and more alive and give us something to talk about when around others, making us more interesting to be with.

Important: Consult in advance with your tax adviser regarding any tax issues, financial adviser regarding financial issues, attorney regarding legal issues, and your physician regarding physical activities and health issues.

The Joy of Giving Back

WHAT DO YOU enjoy doing? What would you like to try? How can you make a difference?

While working a full-time job, it can be very difficult to find any time to be able to give back. Once you are retired, you have more time to do the things that have real meaning to you and at the same time allow you to give back to the community. Think about what you have a passion for. It may be children, animals, other seniors, or just about anything. Not only can giving back feel great, but it can also create greater meaning to your life while helping others.

Here are a few ideas:

- Mentor a troubled child
- Tutor children and/or adults

- Volunteer for a "help a senior" program
- Daycare for single working parents
- Animal volunteer programs
- Volunteer at a school
- Help to build a home with Habit for Humanity

Seek out opportunities to do good. Don't wait to be asked. It feels great to extend yourself and help others in need.

Habitat for Humanity

Maintaining Quality of Life as You Age: Putting Yourself on "Retirement Autopilot"

"Retirement autopilot" means that things will run on their own in the way you need them to with little to no work or input on your part.

As time passes, it may become more difficult to manage your finances and other areas of your life. As we age, change can become more and more difficult. There may be things you can do now, while your mind is sharp and you are able to make good decisions for yourself, to enable you to maintain your independence as long as possible

Simplify Your Finances

There are probably many things you can do to simplify your life. The simpler it is, the easier it will be for you to manage it on your own. Consider the following steps.

Consolidate Your Financial Relationships

We've all heard the rule to not put all our eggs in one basket. This rule still applies. What I am talking about here is consolidating your financial relationships and accounts including bank accounts, investments held at financial institutions, plans held at work, dividend-reinvestment plans, and others. I am not saying you need to sell anything. Just have them consolidated into fewer statements. One bank or credit union, one credit card, and one or two investment firms are all that you may really need.

By having fewer relationships, you can reduce the paperwork you receive, reduce getting tax reporting from multiple firms, and have fewer financial statements to manage.

Clean Up Small Accounts

Over time, you may have received a small amount of stock in a company you never purchased, due to a stock split. You may have withdrawn most of your funds at a bank or other financial institution and have kept a minimal amount there to keep the account open. Consider closing these small accounts to make ongoing management of your portfolio easier.

Direct Payment of Bills

Have as many of your regular bills as possible set up on autopay. Your electricity, television, Internet, insurance, phone, and many other bills can be set up to be paid automatically by your credit card.

You will still get a monthly statement to be able to manage your account and charges, but you will no longer have to remember to pay these bills. It may seem like a minor thing right now, but if you get in the habit of bills being paid automatically, when you are older and having difficulty with memory or writing due to arthritis or for any other reason, you can feel secure knowing that the difficulty will not keep you from being able to maintain your independence, because all the bills will still be paid on time.

If you have a credit card that provides points for every dollar you charge, then you may also get a lot of points that you are not getting now. You can use these points to buy things for yourself and for others.

You may also be able to have your credit card paid directly out of your checking or savings account. You will want to be sure to monitor your checking/savings account to ensure there is a sufficient balance to cover the payment. I suggest you put an average of three months of expected charges in your checking account and every two months make any needed adjustments.

The more bills you can have set up as direct pay, the better it can be. This can

- keep you from having to write a check;
- save you the cost of postage, envelopes, and checks; and
- prevent you from forgetting to pay the bill.

Quarterly Estimated Federal and/or State Income Tax Payments

If you have a pension, Social Security, or qualified plan that you are receiving income from, then you may never need to make quarterly estimated income tax payments. Work with your tax adviser to adjust the withholding from your income sources so that the correct amount of tax is withheld, and you no longer have to remember every three months how much to make the checks out for, where to mail them, and how much a stamp costs.

You will want to review the amount with your tax adviser once a year at tax time or sooner if you have any major income or deductible expense changes to see if any adjustments to the amount need to be made.

Cost Basis

If you ever need to sell a mutual fund, stock, and most all other investments that have the ability to appreciate and are not located in a retirement plan, then you will need to know the cost basis to prove the amount of the sale that you are not required to pay income tax on. This will be less of an issue going forward, because companies are now required to keep track of "cost basis" for you. Cost basis is the amount of the sale of an appreciated security that you do not have to pay income tax on. It is the difference between the amount you paid for the investment plus all reinvested earnings and reinvested capital gains compared to the value received at the time it is sold.

For investments you purchased before the law went into effect, you will need to have a record of the cost basis yourself. The change in the law started in 2011 for some investments and included others over the next five years.

Example:

- You invested $10,000 in a stock or mutual fund.

- Over the years, $3,000 of dividends and capital gains were reinvested to purchase additional shares.

- You sell the investment today for $18,000 (the higher value is due to the increased price per share of the investment).

In this example, your cost basis is $13,000 ($10,000 purchase price plus $3,000 reinvested capital gains and dividends). You would pay income tax on $5,000.

If you do not have the cost basis for each investment, then a good place to start is to ask the company that holds the investment. Until recently, investment companies and banks were not required to keep track of this for you, but they still may be able to help. For a fee, some firms will offer to provide you with all your past statements so you can add it all up yourself or have your tax adviser or financial adviser help you add it up.

Obtaining this information now while your mind is sharp and you do not need to sell anything can make it a lot easier for you later when you may need the money for your own care, an emergency, or for any other reason.

Credit Cards and Charge Accounts

Consider consolidating all your credit cards to only one low-interest card. Cut up the other cards and send a letter to the credit card companies requesting that your account be closed. Once again, this will reduce the amount of paperwork you receive and will make managing your finances much simpler.

Income in Respect of a Decedent

During our working years, many people tend to place their money in tax-deferred investments to avoid paying income tax on it while their tax rate may be high. By the time they retire, the bulk of their assets may be in tax-deferred positions.

A frequently overlooked tax that can occur at death is the tax on income in respect of a decedent (IRD). This is an income tax that beneficiaries of tax-deferred investments must pay. Some of the investments subject to the IRD tax are shown below:

- Qualified plans (401[k] and the like)
- Individual retirement accounts (IRAs)
- Tax-deferred annuities
- Certain government bonds
- Deferred compensation benefits

These are dollars that have never been taxed. And although at death you or your surviving spouse may have the ability to roll the money to your/his/her own retirement plan to keep the assets tax deferred, your heirs may have a large income tax to pay. Assuming these assets continue to grow, even with your required distributions from your qualified plans, your heirs may have a substantially higher income tax to pay.

Talk to your estate planning attorney, tax adviser, and financial adviser about the best option for you to help lower or avoid this tax.

A Few Tips on Managing Money in Retirement

SPLIT YOUR INCOME SOURCES INTO TWO CATEGORIES—NECESSARY AND DISCRETIONARY

Necessary expenses include heat, electricity, telephone, water, sewer, insurance, mortgage/rent, food, clothes, and other mandatory expenses.

Discretionary expenses are not necessary but make life more comfortable, happy, and enjoyable. This includes vacations, entertainment, hobbies, dining out, gift giving, sports, and other expenses that are not a necessity.

Keep in mind that it is important in retirement to have a properly diversified investment portfolio. Securing your income in retirement may be more important than securing your principle. For example, is it more important that you have $100,000 invested that guarantees your principle even if it provides only less than 1 percent income? Or is it better to have a $75,000 investment that provides 4 percent income?

Although growth-oriented investments are not guaranteed and can be riskier, they typically offer greater potential return. This increased return potential is important to help keep up with inflation, including the rising cost of medical care.

Because necessary expenses are mandatory, consider positioning your assets so that your necessary expenses are covered by secure income sources such as pension, Social Security, and secure investment income.

You have more control over your discretionary expenses. If interest rates decline or the market is down, you can adjust your discretionary expenses but not your necessary expenses. Therefore, it may be better to position your variable investments to pay for your discretionary expenses.

Your financial adviser can help you determine and position the right balance of secure and variable assets for your risk tolerance, time frame, income need, tax situation, and other important factors that should be taken into consideration.

Paying Off Your Debt When Planning Retirement or During Retirement

It may feel more comfortable to withdraw a lump sum of money and pay off debt when planning retirement or during retirement. Often, that is not a good idea, especially when debt interest rates are low. Think of it this way: if you take a lump sum and pay off low-interest debt, the lump sum is gone forever as well as the long-term income it can provide. Odds are, you will not replace it. If you continue to make the payments, eventually the debt will be paid off, and you will still have the lump sum to throw off income for the rest of your life.

Consider a Reverse Mortgage

If you really want to stay in your home and find it financially impossible to do so, a reverse mortgage may be an option. A reverse mortgage allows you to access a portion of the equity in your home to cover current income or lump sum needs. I strongly suggest this should only be used as a last resort as a reverse mortgage is typically very expensive. Consult with your financial adviser and attorney to be sure this is the best option for you and that you have exhausted all other less expensive options first.

Handle Your Medical Expenses and Income Taxes

Here is an example of a strategy that can be helpful for many people with high medical expenses.

As Bernice was getting older, she needed more medical care, and although she had health insurance, many of her expenses were not covered. Instead of using already-taxed money to pay these expenses, she withdrew from her retirement plans in an amount equal to the tax-deductible expense. If she had to pay $2,000 out of pocket, she withdrew $2,000 from her retirement plan with no income tax withheld. This was extremely helpful for many reasons. First, she paid no income tax on the withdrawal because her medical expenses offset it. Second, instead of spending her already-taxed money leaving her only taxable assets to access later, she left the tax-free money available. Third, at her death, the taxable assets have already been reduced, saving her heirs a lot of money and at no cost to Bernice.

Passwords and Frequent-Flyer Numbers

Give a list of all your passwords and frequent-flyer numbers to a trusted family member, and keep the list up to date. Another option may be to leave it in a safe or safe deposit box, being sure your trusted family member has access.

If you become ill and need assistance managing your affairs or if you die prematurely, it is important for someone else to have this information. He or she may need your passwords to access information for you when you need assistance, and after you are gone, he or she will want to close the accounts to avoid identity theft including the potential access to financial assets before your estate is settled.

Most airlines will allow frequent flyer mileage to be transferred to a spouse at death. It will be helpful for them to have your frequent-flyer numbers so they can more easily request the transfer.

How Long to Keep Important Documents

Most experts suggest saving every tax-related document (including relevant receipts and canceled checks) for seven years after you file the return. Aside from that, opinions differ. Here are reasonable guidelines:

- Keep pay stubs and canceled personal checks for one year, then shred and discard those that you won't need for tax, warranty, or insurance purposes.
- Shred all credit card, debit card, and ATM receipts after you have checked the transactions against your monthly statements except those you are saving for tax purposes. It is a major deterrent to criminals stealing your identity. You can purchase an inexpensive shredder at many department and office supply stores.
- Before discarding, shred all statements from your health plan and anything that bears

your signature, credit account number, land line or cell phone number, Social Security number, or medical or legal information.

- Keep store receipts until you are sure you won't need to return or exchange the item. Receipts for items that have warranties should be attached to the warranty information and saved in case you need proof of purchase later. Also, save receipts for items that may relate to your current insurance or taxes.

- Supporting tax documentation, such as receipts, W-2s, 1099s, canceled checks, and credit card statements can generally be shredded three years after the return's due date. In some special circumstances, however, you may need to hold on to tax documentation longer. Consult a qualified tax adviser for more information.

- Keep warranty cards, instructions, and receipts for high-ticket items for as long as you own the item.

- Keep canceled checks and invoices for any permanent home improvements until you sell your house.
- Store car maintenance records until you sell the car, at which time, you should give them to the new owner. Keep the purchase order and title for as long as you own the vehicle.
- Keep records of the purchase and sale of mutual funds and stocks until you've reported the transactions to the Internal Revenue Service, and then keep the records with your other tax-related documents. Consult a qualified tax adviser for more information.

Some of the documents that should be kept permanently in a fireproof box, safe deposit box, or home fireproof safe include the following:

- Birth and marriage certificates
- College transcripts, diplomas

- Credit card and loan agreements
- Divorce decree and property agreements
- Mortgage documents
- Home inventory
- Insurance policies
- Passport (current)
- Pension plan and retirement plan documents
- Social Security cards
- Stock purchase agreements
- Tax returns
- Will, living will, power of attorney, and trusts
- Home deed
- Automobile title
- Other important documents

It is important to note that just because a storage box or safe says it is fireproof, it doesn't necessarily mean your items are safe.

When a safe is listed as fireproof, it typically means fire cannot get into the box. Just as important is how much heat it can handle and for how long. If the fire is hotter or lasts longer than the safe is rated for, the fire may not get in, but when you open it, all of your documents could be ashes.

Before you purchase a fireproof storage container or safe, check the fire endurance and degrees listed for how secure your items will be.

Addressing all of this while you are able will not only be much easier on you, but it will be easier on those who will need to later help you.

Your Credit Report-Free Annual Credit Report

Check your credit report annually. Even if you do not plan on needing credit, it is important that you know what your report says about you and that it is accurate. You can receive a free credit report by contacting the service outlined below:

By Phone: Call: 1-877-322-8228

By Mail: Annual Credit Report Request Service

PO Box 105281, Atlanta, GA 30348–50281

By Internet: www.annualcreditreport.com

Important: Consult in advance with your tax adviser regarding any tax issues, financial adviser regarding financial issues, attorney regarding legal issues, and your physician regarding physical activities and health issues.

Health and Wellness

As we age, maintaining our health and wellness can become more challenging.

There are many things you can do to help maintain your quality of life as it relates to your physical and mental health.

Of course, you should consult with your doctor regarding your plan to maintain your health and wellness. And this is the first place to start.

Get in the habit of seeing your doctor, dentist, eye care professional, hearing care professional, and any other professionals at their recommended time schedule for you. If you have not seen any of these professionals in a year, make an appointment now to have a complete checkup.

Maintaining your health and wellness are imperative to be able to live your life to the fullest. Do everything you can to remain active and physically and emotionally fit.

Medical Information

Although medical technology requirements today are making it easier to keep track of your medical history and current medications, for now, you should still keep track of them yourself. Consider keeping an up-to-date list of your medical information including your name, address, name and quantity of each medication you take; name, address, and phone number of all of your doctors; list of any allergies; name of each medical condition; name and dates of any shots you have received; date of any surgeries you have had; and any other important information.

Also, include whom to contact in the event of an emergency and a list of your medical insurance and prescription insurance information. Set up a document on your computer to manage the information. Put the date at the top of the page, and change the date any time you make a change to the information. That way, you will know if you have the most up-to-date page with you. I suggest you carry this in your wallet. I carry this with me at all times and also carry the same for my spouse. That way, I can help him when needed.

Long-Term Care

Maintaining our independence as we age while at the same time ensuring the appropriate level of quality care we need is imperative. If you could no longer fully care for yourself, have you planned how you will pay for the care you need? I am not talking about medical expenses that your health insurance will pay for. I am talking about the help you may need to dress, bathe, manage your medications, cook, clean, and any other task that becomes too difficult for you to manage on your own.

Many families today need the income from both spouses working to support their family. They are not able to take off work to help care for their parents. They also may not have the medical skills or physical strength needed. Therefore, relying on your family or others to care for you may not be a reasonable option.

There have been major changes in the options available over the last twenty or more years to assist with the high costs of care.

Long-term care insurance has been evolving and offers more cost-effective options today than it did in the past. Most long-term care insurance plans will pay to have someone care for you in your own home or an assisted living facility and not just in a nursing home.

Keep in mind, as with other insurance coverages, you cannot wait until you need it to apply for coverage. Researching coverage options now will ensure a lower price than when you are older. Also, keep in mind that if you wait, you run the risk of no longer being insurable if your health changes. Talk to your financial adviser or insurance professional now to determine if long term care insurance is an appropriate option for you and your spouse.

Medications and Stored Food

At least quarterly, go through all medications and monthly for stored food, and throw away everything that is outdated. This will help ensure you will not accidently take a medication or eat or drink something that will hurt you.

Don't Stress About It

Remember the old saying "Accept the things you cannot change, change the things you can, and have the wisdom to know the difference." Learn to let go when you should, but hold on to what you believe when appropriate. Don't worry about what others think of you. Life is much too short to sweat the small stuff. Now is the time to really enjoy your life.

Home Sweet Home Today, Tomorrow, and…

WHAT CONDITION IS your home in? Does it need repair now? Will it need repair in the next twenty years? Can you maintain it on your own today as well as five years from now? Will you be able to maintain it ten, fifteen, or twenty years from now? If you could no longer manage stairs, would you be able to live in your current home comfortably?

Answering these questions now while you are not forced to do so can enable you to make the best decisions for yourself and convey it to others appropriately so they will know how to best help you when the time comes.

If you can stay in your current home long term, make changes now to make it easier and more comfortable as you age to be able to live in your own home as long as possible.

Changes to Make Staying at Home Easier and Comfortable for the Long Term

INSTALL OR UPDATE A HOME SECURITY SYSTEM

The main reason to invest in a security system is to deter crime in your home. According to the Electronic Security Association's "Home Safety Fast Facts" report, nine out of ten burglars said that if they encountered an alarm or home security system, they would not attack the home. According to the Greenwich Study of Residential Security report, homes without a security system are 2.7 to 3.5 times more likely to be burglarized.

Installing a security system in your home can give you and your family greater peace of mind regarding your safety.

GET AN AUTOMATIC GENERATOR

Some areas of the country experience power outages fairly often. If you live in one of those areas, an automatic generator can be extremely important for your health and safety. An automatic generator is one that comes on and runs automatically when the power goes out, unlike a portable generator that you have to hook up and continually add fuel to keep it running. With an automatic generator, you will be able to ensure heat, air conditioning, electricity, and other important services are not interrupted.

DECLUTTER YOUR HOME

As we age, many people tend to accumulate more and more items. There are many reasons for you to thin out and organize your home now. Clutter can make it more difficult to get around and increases the risk of falls. Also, it can be more difficult to find things when you need them. When you can no longer live in your home, the task may be overwhelming. If you later need someone else to do it for you, he or she will not know what is important to you to keep and what he or she can remove from your home. It is not fair for you to leave a mess for someone else to deal with. Clean out and organize all closets, the basement, the attic, all drawers, and each room in general.

Remove obstacles in the house that could cause tripping—everything from small floor rugs to objects on the floor such as an oversized vase or magazine stand.

To make the task less overwhelming, take one area at a time and set a schedule for which areas you will do and when. It may take only a few days, or it may take a year. In any case, the longer you wait, the more difficult of a task it may become.

Sort things into sections: things to donate, things to throw away, things to save, things to give to others, and maybe things to go in a tag sale. When you donate items to charity, be sure to obtain a receipt. You may then be able to deduct the current value on your income taxes to save money.

Just as important is the fact that you will be the person to decide what stays in the home and what goes instead of someone else making that decision for you.

Ask for help or hire a professional to help you if needed.

Make the Home Easier to Live in and More Organized

- For every item that comes in, one needs to leave. You have only a certain amount of space at home. Set a rule for yourself that for every item you bring into the house, something else of similar or larger volume has to leave. For example, it's okay to buy a new outfit, but you have only so much closet space. So, when you bring in a new outfit, remove another outfit from your wardrobe and from your home.

- Color code and label storage. To make it easier to find things, store them in color-coded bins. For example, Christmas items in red and green containers and Halloween items in black and orange containers. Label the outside of every container with what is inside. Colorful containers can be found at most department stores close to the time of each holiday or online.

- Put in a ramp. If needed, put in a ramp to allow easier access to enter and exit your home.

- Install grab bars. Installing grab bars in the bathroom and other areas where needed will assist you in maintaining safe mobility within your home.

- Place nonslip mats on the shower and bathtub floors to help avoid falls.

- Install handrails and lights on staircases, with light switches at the top and bottom of the stairs.

- Paint doorsills with a different, highlighting color to avoid tripping.

- Stove knobs. Purchase a stove that has the control knobs on the front rather than in the back. Having knobs on the back of the stove can be very dangerous. To turn off a hot burner, you have to reach over the heat to turn it off. There are many fires each year caused by a dangling sleeve catching on fire and other accidental burns and fires.

- Door and faucet handle. Change out all knobs to levers. This includes doors, faucets, and any other knobs. As we age, arthritis can make it very difficult to turn a knob. A lever can be much easier to manage.

- Carpet padding. Falls tend to happen more often as we age. To help minimize injury, install double-thick padding under all carpeting. You can do this the next time you replace your carpeting. Or instead, don't wait and do it now to help avoid an injury before it happens.

- Purchase appliances that turn off automatically. Our memories can be less efficient as we age. Having certain appliances turn off automatically, such as an iron, electric heaters, fans, and the like is another way to better ensure your safety.

- Higher wattage lightbulbs. Change all lightbulbs to a higher wattage within the acceptable range for each receptacle. Keeping the home well-lit is another way to reduce the potential for falls and better ensure you can see well in your home. The small amount of increased cost for electricity is well worth it because it may keep you from being seriously injured.

- Install motion-sensor lights around the house. Installing motion-sensor lights that turn on automatically when you enter a room will light your way and help you maintain safe mobility within your home.

- Identity theft. Unfortunately, identity theft has become much more of an issue in recent years. Criminals can now copy your credit card and other personal information even when you have them hidden in your wallet or purse by using special concealed electronic devices. You can now purchase sleeves to put your credit cards in, travel bags, wallets, and other items that have radio frequency identification (RFI) blocking embedded in them. When your personal data is encased in RFI-blocking material, it is not penetrable by this equipment. For greater security, be sure all of your credit cards and other important data are encased in RFI-blocking material. You can find this online and at many local department or travel stores.

- Shred documents. As mentioned earlier, when you are throwing documents away that have your personal information, account numbers, passwords, or other identifying data, be sure to shred them.

- Applications for your smartphone. Consider apps that are available to make your life easier. Here are two free apps to consider:
  - Care Zone. With this app, you can keep track of all of your medications. You will then have easy access to a list of all of your medications, dosage, the date the prescription expires, and other important information whenever you need it.
  - Key Ring. You no longer have to have all those store rewards cards attached to your key chain. Key Ring stores your reward card numbers for you. When you are at the checkout, just show the cashier the information on your smartphone.

Using Online Resources

The Internet has become an amazing resource for people of every age but especially for seniors and people with disabilities or illness. Below are a few of the many options available to help make life easier and help you maintain your independence.

- Mail order prescriptions. Many prescriptions can now not only be mailed direct to your home, but they can also be set up to ship automatically to you when your supply is low. The company keeps track of how many days of medication you were sent. They know when you will be needing more and ship a supply automatically without you contacting them. Check with your doctor or prescription company for more information.
- Online shopping. When you can't get to the store, you can shop online for just about anything, whether it be for yourself or gifts for others. You are probably already doing this, but did you know the following?
  - You can order gift cards for most restaurants, stores, and other places online.

They will mail them to you, making it easy for you to give as a gift without leaving the house. Go directly to their website or call and ask them if they will do it over the phone and send you a confirmation of your purchase.

- You can also find unique gifts. For example, I researched and found matching sweaters for three children and their parents. That is often impossible to find because they each need to come from a different department, infants, adult male, young girl's department, and so on. Just put in the search bar "matching family sweaters" or whatever you need and see what comes up.

- A great gift option when you don't know what to get someone may be available at chooseyourgift.com. This is a site where you can purchase a booklet that lists a host of different gifts. You choose the price range, and the booklet is mailed to you. When you give the booklet as a gift, the recipient fills out a postage-paid card listing the item he or she has chosen from the booklet, and his or her gift is mailed to him or her postage free.

- Peapod and other food delivery services. Today, you can go online to sites of many local grocery stores, select what you need, and request it to be delivered to your home. They will even keep a list of what you purchased from them in the past and let you know when it is on sale. You no longer have to worry about getting to the store in bad weather or when you don't feel well.

- Birthday and other important event reminders. Online free services such as birthday-reminders.com and others can help you remember important dates like birthdays, anniversaries, and such. Once you set this up, they will send a reminder to your computer prior to the date, so you never have to miss an important event.

- PayPal and other payment processing services. Buying online can be extremely helpful, but giving out your credit card information to unknown sites may not be safe. Consider using PayPal or another reputable payment services. For example, with PayPal, you give it your credit card information. When you make an online purchase with a company that accepts PayPal, your charge is processed through PayPal. The company you are making the purchase with never sees your credit card information. This can be a safer way to make a purchase online.

Internet sites change, and new services are added all the time. Be sure the site you plan to use is reputable and available each time you search for it or use it.

Protection of Your Personal Property

Obtain records and pictures of all household items for casualty insurance purposes. A home inventory is one of the best resources you can have after a disaster or theft. It can help you get your insurance claims processed more easily and can help to lessen your stress level. You can only collect for what you can prove you lost. Include a picture of each item (a videotape can be very effective), its serial number, an appraisal of its worth where appropriate, and any relevant sales receipts. Then keep this inventory somewhere safe such as a fireproof and waterproof safe or safe deposit box. It won't help you much if it is destroyed along with your possessions.

If You Are No Longer Able to Live in Your Current Home, Where Would You Prefer to Live?

Research places now, while you can be the one making the decision. This includes adult individual home communities, assisted living facilities, transitional facilities, and nursing homes. Take notes about what you like and don't like about each place you visited. Weigh the pros and cons, and decide how you feel about each location. Then let your family know what your first, second, and third choices are and where you would not want to be.

Doing this now will better ensure you will be at the place you would feel most comfortable if a location other than your home would be safer and/or better for you. This will also take the burden off others to have to make that choice for you.

Legal Documents

As mentioned earlier in this book, having the proper legal documents in place now can make a major difference when the time comes that you need others to help you and to ensure everything goes to whom you want it to go to as intact as possible after you are gone. It is important that you have the proper documents in place now. If you wait until they are needed, it will most likely be too late.

Do you have the following documents in place? If you do, how often do you have them reviewed and updated by your attorney?

- A will enables you to name who will inherit your assets. And although many assets have the ability for you to name a beneficiary, some do not. For example, you cannot list a beneficiary on the contents of your home including artwork, jewelry, and other valuables. You also cannot name a beneficiary on your home. You can, of course, put someone else as the joint owner of the home, but for many reasons, that may not be appropriate. You may need a will or trust for that.

- A trust is a legal document that gives a person the ability to give another party the right to hold property (real estate, investments, etc.) for the benefit of a third party, the beneficiary.

- A durable power of attorney provides the ability to choose who will make decisions for you (rather than a court) when you are medically unable to do so. It can also avoid the necessity of a guardianship or conservatorship. Moreover, it can provide you and your family members a good opportunity to discuss wishes and desires. It can provide peace of mind for you and anyone who you may need to assist you in the future.

- Health-care powers or living wills and other advance directives are written, legal instructions regarding your preferences for medical care if you are unable to make decisions for yourself. They help guide your choices for doctors and caregivers if you're terminally ill, seriously injured, in a coma, in the late stages of dementia, or near the end of life. By planning ahead, you are better able to get the medical care you want, avoid unnecessary suffering, and relieve caregivers of decision-making burdens during moments of crisis or grief. You also help reduce confusion or disagreement about the choices you would want people to make on your behalf.

Be sure to keep all your documents up to date. Once your documents have been prepared, you should review them with your attorney at least every three years (or sooner if needed) to ensure they are up to date. Remember, even if your situation and goals have not changed, the laws may have changed, making your current plan out of date and therefore no longer providing for or protecting what you had intended.

What You Want/Don't Want Regarding Your Funeral and Assets

WRITE DOWN HOW you want things to be handled after you pass. Be as detailed as you can. Letting your loved ones know what your wishes are can help them a lot at a time that may be very difficult for them. Consider the following:

- Do you want a funeral?
- If you want a funeral, how simple or elaborate do you want it?
- Is there anyone you want the family to notify, such as out-of-town people who may not know you have passed?
- If you want to be buried, where?

- If you want to be cremated, where do you want your ashes to be placed?
- Is there anything else you want the family to know?

Whom to Get Special Items You Possess

I know of many families who have argued over a parent's things after their parent has passed. In some cases, the siblings are so upset that they don't speak for many years, if ever again. You can help ensure that does not happen to your family by making it really clear whom you want to receive your personal possessions. Put it in writing and keep an up-to-date copy in your safe or safe deposit box.

Your investments and insurance should already be covered by the beneficiary designation you placed on each or the trust you have placed your assets in, if you have one. This list is for personal items that you cannot place a beneficiary on, such as the following:

- Each piece of valuable jewelry
- Collections
- Family heirlooms
- Electronics
- Cars
- Boat
- Other

Leave a Note Stating What You Want Your Family to Know

What are the last words you want your family to hear from you? Consider writing a letter to leave behind. It will be something they will always cherish. You can include things such as the following:

- What you like best about each of the people you leave behind
- What your favorite memories are
- What you enjoyed most during your life
- What you want to be remembered for
- Words of advice you want to pass on

Other Things to Address

Register Your Name on the National Do Not Call Registry

HOW MANY TIMES each week do you get sales calls at your home? To help avoid annoying sales calls, you can add your name to the National Do Not Call Registry by contacting them as outlined below:

Phone: call 1-888-382-1222

Internet: to fill out the registration form, visit http://www.donotcall.gov

Forgive Yourself and Others

Forgiveness is good for your body and your soul. Forgiving can be incredibly difficult, but it can also reduce stress, decrease your blood pressure, and lower your heart rate. Forgiveness can help you feel happier even if the other person never acknowledges the wrongdoing.

Be Honest with Yourself and Others

If you need help, get it. It's very important to maintain your independence, but do not ignore the realities. If you cannot safely make it on your own, reach out to family and friends for assistance. Independence may become more difficult as we age, but we still have the freedom to choose our own path.

List All Professionals for Others to Know Whom to Contact When You Need Help

Make a list of all of the professionals who assist you. Include their name, address, telephone number, and specialty. Post a copy on your refrigerator. Some people to consider include the following:

- All doctors
- Dentist
- Eye care professional
- Therapists
- Attorney
- Financial adviser
- Tax adviser
- The person who has your power of attorney
- The person who has your health-care power
- House cleaners
- Handyman
- Insurance agent
- Other

Resources

FOR ADDITIONAL INFORMATION for greater independence, happiness, and success in your senior years, check out these resources.

General Resources

AARP

http://www.aarp.org/

A member organization, AARP provides a host of articles of interest to older adults. Topics range from preventing identity theft to attending graduate school to travel tips. AARP also conducts research and posts its findings online.

ADMINISTRATION ON AGING

http://www.aoa.gov/

The US Administration on Aging is a federal agency. Its site provides information about housing, finances, nutrition, and health. It also introduces elders to senior services and volunteer opportunities.

CIVIC VENTURES

http://www.encore.org/

Civic Ventures is a nonprofit think tank that promotes volunteerism, healthy aging, and innovative approaches to retirement. The site links to related articles and research with particular emphasis on baby boomers.

DEPARTMENT OF VETERANS AFFAIRS

http://www.va.gov/

The official site of the US Department of Veterans Affairs (VA) provides information about health, education, pension, and burial benefits. It offers a process to appeal VA decisions. VA patients can refill prescriptions online and access their health records.

GOOD50

http://www.good50.com/

Good50 is a search engine for seniors and those with low vision. This site was made to help seniors and those with disabilities to have an easier time searching the web.

NATIONAL CENTER ON ELDER ABUSE

http://www.ncea.aoa.gov/

A national resource, this site offers information about the types of abuse, risk factors, and what to do if you suspect abuse or neglect of an older adult. It also provides statistics, surveys, and reports about the problem of abuse.

Health-Related Resources

ALZHEIMER'S ASSOCIATION

http://www.alz.org/

The Alzheimer's Association supports families caring for a loved one with dementia and supports prevention and treatment research. Packed full of excellent information about dementia, this site offers everything from the basics to scientific papers.

AMERICAN CANCER SOCIETY

http://www.cancer.org/

This nonprofit organization presents information about cancer prevention, detection, and treatment. It also offers ways to get involved, donate, or connect with other cancer survivors.

ARTHRITIS FOUNDATION

http://www.arthritis.org/

This nonprofit organization provides information about living with arthritis. Topics include nutrition, preventing injury, and tips for working and traveling. It also presents information about legislation of interest to people with the disease.

GERIATRIC MENTAL HEALTH FOUNDATION

http://www.gmhfonline.org/

Established by the American Association for Geriatric Psychiatry, this site offers information about depression, dementia, and substance abuse for older adults and caregivers.

MEDICARE

http://www.medicare.gov/

The official federal government site for information about Medicare, this site offers information about benefits, appealing Medicare decisions, long-term care, enrollment, and the new drug program.

For Consumers

BENEFITS CHECKUP

http://www.benefitscheckup.org/

Operated by the National Council on Aging, this short questionnaire will help anyone find programs that can assist with rent, property taxes, heating bills, meals, and many other needs. Information on Medicare prescription drug coverage is also available at this site.

NATIONAL FRAUD INFORMATION CENTER
http://www.fraud.org/
Operated by the National Consumers League, this site provides information about telemarketing and Internet fraud. It provides an online form and phone number to report fraud and tips for spotting a scam.

For Caregivers

FAMILY CAREGIVER ALLIANCE
http://www.caregiver.org/
A nonprofit organization, the Family Caregiver Alliance offers a wealth of information about topics of interest to people caring for a loved one. It provides advice about dealing with dementia,

disturbing behaviors, hands-on skills, hiring outside help, and other practical information.

NATIONAL ALLIANCE FOR CAREGIVING
http://www.caregiving.org/
A nonprofit coalition of organizations that help caregivers, the National Alliance for Caregiving offers tips and advice about providing care to a family member. You can download publications about caregiving, leaving the hospital, palliative care, and aiding aging parents.

Your Plan for Success

WHEN YOU ARE at the end of your life looking back, how will you feel about the following?

The life you led
What you accomplished
How you treated others

For whatever years you have left on this earth, do what you can now to put all your ducks in a row so you can feel really great when you are later looking back at your life.

Make every day count!

What to Do Now

First review all the strategies outlined in this book. Then determine what is important to you and which steps you want to take now to help you maintain your independence for the long term and make your life the best it can be.

The following list outlines all of the items included in this book. Use this list to organize your plan for success and track your progress.

Important: Do not put this off. Start now while you are physically and mentally able to do this. Later you will be glad you did, and others who may need to assist you will thank you for taking the time and effort to put everything in order. How you handle things now can help determine your quality of life for the rest of your days.

Evaluate the following and make changes where appropriate:

All money needed for the next five years should not be in the market.

Date Started: _______________________________

Date Completed: _______________________________

Notes:_______________________________

____

Take only the amount of risk you need to accomplish your goals.

Date Started: _______________________________

Date Completed: _______________________________

Notes:_______________________________

____

Check to be sure you are not taking more income than your portfolio can support.

Date Started: _______________________________

Date Completed: _____________________________

Notes:_______________________________________

____

Consider your priorities regarding goal #1 and goal #2.

Date Started: _______________________________

Date Completed: _____________________________

Notes:_______________________________________

____

A gift of "Our Memories of You" slips

Date Started: _______________________________

Date Completed: _____________________________

Notes:_______________________________________

____

Make more family memories; start a new family tradition.

Date Started: _______________________________

Date Completed: _____________________________

Notes:_______________________________________

____

Capture the rich history of senior family members and yourself via video.

Date Started: _______________________________

Date Completed: _____________________________

Notes:_______________________________________

____

Encourage others to take calculated risk for a better life and do something they have never done before.

Date Started:________________________________

Date Completed:______________________________

Notes:_______________________________________

____

Learn something new now, and make learning ongoing.

Date Started:_______________________________________

Date Completed:_____________________________________

Notes:____

____

The joy of giving back—take on a new opportunity to give back.

Date Started: ______________________________________

Date Completed: ____________________________________

Notes:____

____

Consolidate financial relationships.

Date Started: ______________________________________

Date Completed: ____________________________________

Notes:____

____

Clean up small accounts.

Date Started: _______________________________

Date Completed: _______________________________

Notes:_______________________________

____

Set up direct payment of bills.

Date Started: _______________________________

Date Completed: _______________________________

Notes:_______________________________

____

Consider changing withholding to no longer file quarterly tax payments.

Date Started: _______________________________

Date Completed: _______________________________

Notes:_______________________________

____

Obtain all cost basis.

Date Started: _______________________________________

Date Completed: ____________________________________

Notes:____

____

Consolidate charge accounts.

Date Started: _______________________________________

Date Completed: ____________________________________

Notes:____

____

Address income in respect of a descendant, to lower it.

Date Started: _______________________________________

Date Completed: ____________________________________

Notes:____

____

Split your income sources into two categories—necessary and discretionary.

Date Started: _______________________________

Date Completed: _______________________________

Notes:_______________________________

____

Consider not paying off low-interest debt when planning retirement or during retirement.

Date Started: _______________________________

Date Completed: _______________________________

Notes:_______________________________

____

Reverse mortgage—consider all other options first.

Date Started: _______________________________

Date Completed: _______________________________

Notes:_______________________________

____

Consider offsetting tax-deductible medical expenses with qualified plan withdrawals.

Date Started: _______________________________

Date Completed: _____________________________

Notes:_______________________________________

____

Provide access to your list of all passwords and frequent-flyer numbers to a trusted family member.

Date Started: _______________________________

Date Completed: _____________________________

Notes:_______________________________________

____

Review all statements and other identifying documents and shred all that are not needed.

Date Started: _______________________________

Date Completed: _____________________________

Notes:_______________________________________

____

Obtain your credit report now and annually thereafter.

Date Started:_______________________________

Date Completed:_____________________________

Notes:_____________________________________

____

See your doctor, dentist, eye care professional, hearing care professional, and any other professionals at their recommended time schedule for you.

Date Started:_______________________________

Date Completed:_____________________________

Notes:_____________________________________

____

Obtain a list of all medical information, and keep it up to date.

Date Started: ______________________________

Date Completed: ____________________________

Notes:_____________________________________

____

Research purchasing long-term care insurance.

Date Started:______________________________________

Date Completed:___________________________________

Notes:____

____

Review all medication and stored food, and dispose of all that are outdated.

Date Started: _____________________________________

Date Completed: __________________________________

Notes:____

____

Learn to not stress about the things you cannot change.

Date Started:______________________________________

Date Completed:___________________________________

Notes:____

____

Assess the condition of your home and any repairs that may be needed in the next ten years.

Date Started: _______________________________

Date Completed: _______________________________

Notes:_______________________________

____

Assess if you can stay in your home.

- If you can climb stairs
- If you cannot, search now for an alternative location

Date Started: _______________________________

Date Completed: _______________________________

Notes:_______________________________

____

Install a security system in your home.

Date Started: _______________________________

Date Completed: _______________________________

Notes:_______________________________

____

Install an automatic generator.

Date Started: _______________________________________

Date Completed: _____________________________________

Notes:____

____

Declutter every closet and room of your home.

Date Started: _______________________________________

Date Completed: _____________________________________

Notes:____

____

Adapt a policy that for every item that comes into your home, one item needs to leave.

Date Started: _______________________________________

Date Completed: _____________________________________

Notes:____

____

Color code and label all storage.

Date Started: _______________________________________

Date Completed: _____________________________________

Notes:____

____

Put in a ramp if necessary for easier access.

Date Started: _______________________________________

Date Completed: _____________________________________

Notes:____

____

Install grab bars in the bathroom.

Date Started: _______________________________________

Date Completed: _____________________________________

Notes:____

____

Place nonslip mats on the tub and shower floors.

Date Started: _______________________________

Date Completed: _______________________________

Notes:_______________________________

____

Install handrails and lights on staircases.

Date Started: _______________________________

Date Completed: _______________________________

Notes:_______________________________

____

Paint door sills a contrasting color.

Date Started: _______________________________

Date Completed: _______________________________

Notes:_______________________________

____

Purchase a stove with all knobs in the front.

Date Started: ______________________________

Date Completed: ______________________________

Notes:______________________________

____

Change all handles and knobs to levers.

Date Started: ______________________________

Date Completed: ______________________________

Notes:______________________________

____

Install extra-thick padding under carpeting.

Date Started: ______________________________

Date Completed: ______________________________

Notes:______________________________

____

Purchase appliances that turn off automatically.

Date Started: _______________________________

Date Completed: _____________________________

Notes:______________________________________

____

Change lightbulbs to higher wattage (under maximum allowed).

Date Started: _______________________________

Date Completed: _____________________________

Notes:______________________________________

____

Install motion-sensor lights.

Date Started: _______________________________

Date Completed: _____________________________

Notes:______________________________________

____

Purchase RFI sleeves, wallet, or purse for greater security.

Date Started: _______________________________

Date Completed: _______________________________

Notes:_______________________________

____

Research apps for your smartphone to help organize your life.

Date Started: _______________________________

Date Completed: _______________________________

Notes:_______________________________

____

Discuss with your prescription company and/or doctor, the ability for you to have your prescriptions refilled and sent to you automatically.

Date Started: _______________________________

Date Completed: _______________________________

Notes:_______________________________

____

Online shopping—check out www.chooseyourgift.com and other sites to obtain unique gifts without leaving your home.

Date Started: _______________________________

Date Completed: _____________________________

Notes:______________________________________

____

Research Peapod and other food delivery services so you can use them whenever needed.

Date Started: _______________________________

Date Completed: _____________________________

Notes:______________________________________

____

Consider using an online reminder service for birthdays, anniversaries, and other important dates.

Date Started: _______________________________

Date Completed: _______________________________

Notes:_______________________________

____

Use PayPal or other payment processing services when you make online purchases.

Date Started: _______________________________

Date Completed: _______________________________

Notes:_______________________________

____

Be sure the Internet sites you use are reputable.

Date Started: _______________________________

Date Completed: _______________________________

Notes:_______________________________

____

Obtain records and pictures or all household items.

Date Started:_______________________________

Date Completed:_____________________________

Notes:______________________________________

____

Keep all important documents in a fireproof box, safe deposit box, or home fireproof safe with an appropriate rating for fire endurance.

Date Started:_______________________________

Date Completed:_____________________________

Notes:______________________________________

____

In the event you are no longer able to live in your home, research now where you would prefer to be while you can be the one making the decision.

Date Started: _______________________________

Date Completed: _____________________________

Notes:______________________________________

____

Meet with your attorney and discuss all necessary legal documents. Be sure to review them with your attorney at least every three years.

- Will
- Trust
- Power of attorney
- Health-care power

Date Started: _______________________________________

Date Completed: ____________________________________

Notes:____

____

Write down how you want things handled after you die.

Date Started:_______________________________________

Date Completed:_____________________________________

Notes:____

____

Write down whom you want to receive each of your personal valuable possessions.

Date Started:_______________________________________

Date Completed:_____________________________________

Notes:____

____

Write a note to your family stating what you want them to know after you die.

Date Started:___________________________________

Date Completed:________________________________

Notes:____

____

Register your name on the National Do Not Call Registry.

Date Started:___________________________________

Date Completed:________________________________

Notes:____

____

Forgive yourself and others.

Date Started:___________________________________

Date Completed:________________________________

Notes:____

____

Ask for help whenever you need it.

Date Started:_______________________________________

Date Completed:_____________________________________

Notes:____

____

Make a list of all professionals, doctor, dentist, attorney, and so forth.

Date Started: ______________________________________

Date Completed: ____________________________________

Notes:____

____

Recognize that life is a journey, not a destination. Don't let fear keep you from living a full life. Take calculated risk and step out of your comfort zone. At least weekly, make a point of finding something new and exciting, and go out and experience it.

What you want to experience: _______________

____

Date each is scheduled: ___________________

____

Notes: _________________________________

____

Important: Consult in advance with your tax adviser regarding any tax issues, financial adviser regarding financial issues, attorney regarding legal issues, and physician regarding physical activities and health issues.

Questions to Consider for "Our Memories of You"

Childhood and Family

- Let's start at the beginning. What is your earliest memory?
- I'd like to know about your childhood. What is your happiest childhood memory?
- What were you like as a child?
- What did you want to be when you grew up?
- What did you do for fun as a child?
- What were you like as a teenager?
- Most teenagers do something outrageous or "naughty." What outrageous things did you do?

- Tell me about your school years. What did the schoolhouse/room look like? How did you get to school?
- What did you do during the summer as a child? Did you have favorite games? A favorite doll or toy?
- What chores did you do as a child?
- How were you disciplined as a child?
- Did you have any special pets?
- Tell me about some rites of passage—that is, your first bicycle, your first time shaving, wearing stockings, your bat mitzvah/communion, your first date, and so forth?
- Did you have a teen idol?
- Did you move around growing up? Tell me about the houses you grew up in.
- Who was your best friend growing up?
- Did you ever run away from home?
- In your young adult life, what transportation did you reply on?

- What were some rituals (family traditions) during your childhood?
- Who were you named after?
- What were the dress fashions when you were a teenager?
- What were your favorite clothes as a child, teenager, and young woman/young man?
- Tell me about your parents and siblings.
- Do you remember any funny stories about your parents or siblings?
- Tell me about your hometown.
- What were some of the "old-fashioned" remedies for illness that you remember your parents using?
- Where are your ancestors from? Tell me about them.
- Tell me about a fond memory of your grandparents.
- What was the best advice your parents ever gave you?
- Who was the best teacher you ever had?

Work

- Tell me about your first job. Salary? Experiences?
- What did you like best about your work life?
- What did your work mean to you?
- If you had to start over and choose a different profession or role in life, what would it be?

Religion

- Did you go to synagogue/church?
- What part has religion played in your life?
- What are your favorite religious traditions and holidays?
- Do you believe in heaven and hell?
- Do you believe in God?
- Tell me about your most memorable Hanukkah/Christmas.

- Did you ever have a near-death experience? Tell me about it.
- Do you believe you have a guardian angel?
- Do you believe there is a life after death?

Dating and Marriage

- How did you meet Dad/Mom? What attracted you to him/her?
- What qualities did/do you admire in Dad/Mom?
- Who was your first love?
- Tell me about your first kiss.
- How did Dad/Mom propose to you?
- Tell me about your engagement. How? Where? When?
- What was your family's reaction to your engagement to Dad/Mom?
- Tell me about your wedding day.
- What was your wedding night like?

- Did anything go wrong on your wedding day?
- What was the most romantic event you shared with Dad/Mom?
- How do you feel about premarital sex?
- What factors contributed to a long-lasting, happy marriage?
- What was the one thing that bugged you most about Dad/Mom?
- If you could, what would you do differently in your marriage?
- Where did you go on your honeymoon?
- What was your relationship with your in-laws?
- Tell me about the first house you bought. How much did it cost?

Being a Parent and Grandparent

- What were your thoughts when you learned you were pregnant?

- As a parent, what were the births of your children like? At home or hospital? Doctor or midwife? Who was present?

- How did you choose your children's names?

- What quality do you most admire in each of your children?

- What values have you tried to pass on to your children?

- Tell me about your children. Was raising children an easy or difficult task?

- You stayed at home with your children most of the time. Do you wish you could have worked outside the home?

- What's the funniest (worst, most trying, most rewarding) experience in raising your children?

- Do you wish you had more children?

- As a parent, what is your advice on raising children?

- Tell me about a memorable family trip.

- How are your children like you? How are they different?
- Tell me about your grandchildren.
- What's the best part of being a grandparent?
- Are there any special stories about your children/grandchildren that you'd like to share?

History

- What important historical event do you remember, and what were you doing that day?
- Who was the most famous person you ever met?
- What famous person from your era did you most admire? Why?
- What important historical events do you remember, and how did you feel about them?

- You have seen a lot of changes. What do you wish had not changed?
- A lot has been invented during your life-time—from the radio to Internet. What modern convenience do you most admire? Why?
- Did you ever experience racism, sexism, or ageism?
- What do you consider nature's greatest gift to humankind?
- Who was the first president you voted for?
- What was it like to live in the Depression?
- What was life like during World War II?
- Do you remember a time when you stood up for your rights?
- Did you ever walk a picket line or take part in a demonstration or sit-in?
- If you could go back in time, whom would you most want to see and what would you say to him or her?

- If you ruled the world, what changes would you make?
- What do you think was the most important event during your lifetime? Why?

Life

- Tell me about one of the happiest days of your life.
- Tell me about the hardest thing you ever faced.
- We all have regrets. What is your major regret?
- What is the single event that taught you an important lesson? What was the lesson?
- What is your greatest pet peeve?
- Who were your mentors? What did they teach you?
- What is your greatest accomplishment?
- What decade of life did you most enjoy? Why?

- Tell me about your most memorable illness.
- What is your greatest passion in life?
- What is the best thing that happened in your life?
- What was the biggest disappointment for you?
- What person made you laugh the most?
- What do you wish you had learned to do?
- What gift did you cherish the most of all the gifts you were given?
- Tell me about an embarrassing moment.
- Recall a funny experience you had.
- Was there ever a time when you felt your life was in danger?
- Have you ever gone skinny-dipping? Tell me about it.
- Who was the most influential person in your life?
- What is the hardest thing about being a widow(er)?
- Have you ever saved anyone's life?
- Has anyone ever saved yours?

- What organizations did you belong to?
- What sports and activities did you partici-pate in?
- Tell us about your most memorable vacation.
- Tell us what money meant to you. Were you a saver? Did money come easily or did you have some years of struggling?
- What was the most meaningful reward you received?
- Did you ever lie about your age?
- What is your recipe for a happy, successful life?

Today and for the Rest of Your Life

- You are ___ years old. What's the best part of being your age now?
- What's the hardest part of being your age now?

- What is your most cherished material possession?
- What would you consider a perfect day?
- What do you want to be most remembered for?
- Tell me how you feel about retirement.
- Is there something you always wanted to do but didn't?
- What would you still like to accomplish?
- If you had your life to live over, what one thing would you do differently?
- What is your favorite food/music/art/movie/flower/color?
- Whom do you admire the most now? Why?
- What is your favorite tradition presently?
- If you could invent something to help humankind, what would it be?
- If you had three wishes, what would you wish for?
- In what ways has life been good to you?

- What's the one thing that can make you smile when you're feeling down?
- What is your philosophy of life?
- What is the most valuable life lesson that you would like to pass on to others?
- What would be the greatest news you could receive?
- What advice would you give to the younger generation?
- If money were no object, what would you buy?
- How do you feel about dying?
- How do you want things handled at the time of your death?
- What has surprised you the most in your life?
- What do you like to do now, just for fun?
- What would be your dream vacation?
- Where would you love to travel that you've never visited?

- What do you think about most now?
- What are you most looking forward to now?
- What makes you sad?
- What is the first thing you tell yourself in the morning?
- What is the last thing you tell yourself before you go to sleep?
- What age would you like to live to?
- What is the best part of your day now?
- What are you most grateful for?
- Tell me your favorite joke.
- What one thing would you like to change about yourself?
- What do you like the best about yourself?
- What don't we know about you?
- What can your children do for you now?
- How can we help you live a more comfortable life as you get older?
- As we finish this interview, what would you like us to remember for the rest of our lives?

Life's a Journey...Make It What You Want It to Be.

WHEN YOU ARE at the end of your life looking back, how will you feel about the life you lived, what you have accomplished, and how you treated others?

Use the information in this book starting today to ensure that for whatever years you have left on this earth, you will be able to look back and feel great about how you lived your life today and for the rest of your life. Your future and your happiness are in your hands.